T0337558

# Helen Keller

## Kitson Jazynka

NATIONAL GEOGRAPHIC

Washington, D.C.

Published by Collins
An imprint of HarperCollins*Publishers*
The News Building
1 London Bridge Street
London
SE1 9GF

Browse the complete Collins catalogue at
**www.collins.co.uk**

In association with National Geographic
Partners, LLC

NATIONAL GEOGRAPHIC and the Yellow
Border Design are trademarks of the National
Geographic Society, used under license.

Second edition 2018
First published 2017

ISBN 978-0-00-831727-0

10 9 8 7 6 5 4 3 2

A catalogue record for this book is available from
the British Library

Printed and bound in China by RR Donnelley APS

If you would like to comment on any aspect of
this book, please contact us at the above address
or online.
natgeokidsbooks.co.uk
cseducation@harpercollins.co.uk

Paper from responsible sources

Since 1888, the National Geographic Society has
funded more than 12,000 research, exploration,
and preservation projects around the world. The
Society receives funds from National Geographic
Partners, LLC, funded in part by your purchase.
A portion of the proceeds from this book
supports this vital work. To learn more, visit
http://natgeo.com/info.

**Photo Credits**

# Table of Contents

# Who Was Helen Keller?

Close your eyes and cover your ears with your hands. It's dark and quiet. Can you imagine living in a dark, quiet world all the time?

Helen Keller lived like that. She was blind and deaf, but she didn't let that stop her from learning as much as she could. She used what she learned to help other blind or deaf people have better lives.

This coin has a picture of Helen Keller on it.

Keller (left) often travelled with her assistant, Polly Thomson.

**In Her Own Words**

"Life is either a daring adventure or nothing."

In Keller's time, disabled people were often ignored or sent to live away from their families. Keller worked to change how others thought about disabled people. She wrote articles and books. She travelled the world and spoke out. She inspired disabled people with her courage. She helped change unfair treatment for other people, too.

**Words to Know**

**DISABLED:** Having a condition that limits a person's ability to do something as others do

# Growing Up

Keller was born on June 27, 1880. She lived with her family in the state of Alabama in the USA. When she was about a year and a half old, she became ill with a high fever. Soon she felt better. But she didn't blink when the sun shone in her face. She couldn't hear the dinner bell ring. Doctors said she had lost her sight and hearing forever.

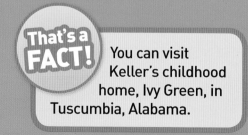

That's a FACT! You can visit Keller's childhood home, Ivy Green, in Tuscumbia, Alabama.

This is the home where Keller grew up.

Keller at age seven

For young Keller, the world had become dark, silent and confusing. Most children learn to speak by hearing and watching others. Keller could do neither. When she tried to speak, no one could understand.

She must have felt lonely and frustrated. She kicked and threw things. Her parents were frustrated, too. But they wouldn't give up on their clever, determined daughter.

At Ivy Green, actors perform *The Miracle Worker*, a play about Keller's life.

# In Her Time

When Keller was a girl in the 1880s, many things were different from how they are today.

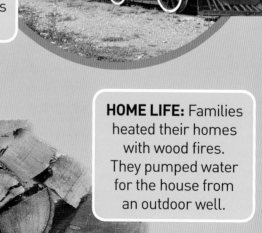

**TRANSPORT:**
People often travelled by train, steamboat, or wagons pulled by horses or oxen.

**HOME LIFE:** Families heated their homes with wood fires. They pumped water for the house from an outdoor well.

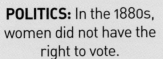
**POLITICS:** In the 1880s, women did not have the right to vote.

**FOOD:** Few people shopped for food. Instead they raised farm animals and grew fruit and vegetables.

**SCHOOL:** Children were taught at home or in one-room schoolhouses. Children of wealthy families might go to boarding schools.

# Learning Letters and Words

A few years later, Keller's mother read about a school for blind and deaf children. There, students learned how to finger-spell words into a person's hands. She wondered if her little girl could learn, too.

This is how to finger-spell the letter *L*. In Keller's time, a blind and deaf person would touch the sign to read it.

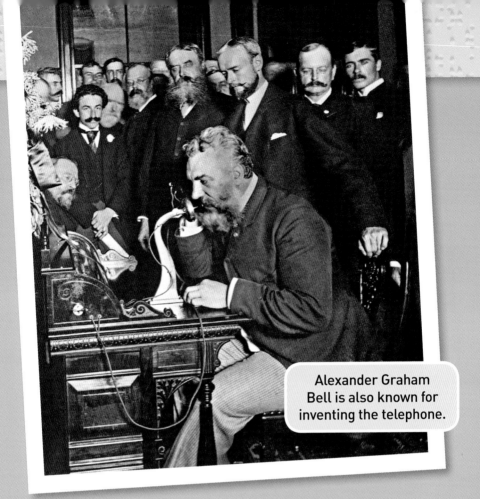

Alexander Graham Bell is also known for inventing the telephone.

Keller and her parents visited Alexander Graham Bell. He was well known for teaching deaf children. Bell helped the Kellers find a teacher for their daughter.

That teacher was Annie Sullivan. She arrived when Keller was six years old. Sullivan finger-spelled words into Keller's hand. But Keller didn't understand.

Keller and her teacher, Annie Sullivan

## Annie Sullivan

Annie Sullivan was 20 years old when she came to live with the Kellers on March 3, 1887. She was partly blind, and she had gone to a school for the blind in Massachusetts, USA. She was smart and stubborn, just like Keller.

The pair worked together for 49 years. Because of her success in helping Keller, Sullivan was called a miracle worker.

Actors show Sullivan pumping water into Keller's hands.

One day, Sullivan finger-spelled "w–a–t–e–r". At the same time, she pumped water onto Keller's other hand. Suddenly Keller understood that the liquid she felt had a name and that Sullivan was spelling it. She danced for joy. She learned 30 more words before bedtime.

Keller couldn't wait to learn more. Within a year, she knew more than 900 words. She mastered braille and typing by the age of 10. Later she went to high school in New York City. Sullivan went with Keller and finger-spelled for her.

### Words to Know

**BRAILLE:** A reading system with raised dots that stand for letters and numbers

a person reading braille

Keller graduated from Radcliffe College in 1904.

At the time, few disabled people went to college. But Keller did. She insisted on the same treatment as other students. With Sullivan's help, she read books and wrote essays.

# 7 COOL FACTS
## About
## Helen Keller

**1**

With Sullivan's help, Keller learned by doing – she rode horses, went swimming and sledding, and touched tadpoles.

In college, Keller learned to read and write French, German and Latin.

**2**

**3**

Keller had a keen sense of vibrations around her and could identify people and pets by their footsteps.

Keller had a special pocket watch with braille features on the outside to tell time with her hands.

**4**

**5**

Keller and Alexander Graham Bell became lifelong friends.

Keller never saw her own face in a mirror.

**6**

**7**

Keller wrote 12 books, as well as many articles for well-known newspapers and magazines.

# Finding Her Voice

By now, many people had heard about Keller, the young blind and deaf woman who could read and write. She did everything she could to help others understand the lives of disabled people. Through writing, she shared her ideas about equal treatment.

### In Her Own Words

"One can never consent to creep when one feels an impulse to soar."

But writing and
finger-spelling were
sometimes too slow for Keller.
She wanted to use her voice to
speak about change.

Helen practised speaking. In 1909, she got help from a singing teacher. A few years later, she was able to give her first speech. She kept practising. She gave more speeches.

She spoke up not only for disabled people, but also for children and the poor. As a suffragette, she spoke up for women, too.

**Words to Know**

**SUFFRAGETTE:** A woman who works for the right of women to vote

| 1880 | 1882 | 1887 |
|---|---|---|
| Born on June 27 in Tuscumbia, Alabama | Suffers an illness that leaves her blind and deaf | Begins work with teacher Annie Sullivan |

That's a FACT! Between 1946 and 1957, Keller spoke in 35 countries on five continents.

**1894**
Attends a school for the deaf in New York City

**1902**
Publishes her first book, *The Story of My Life*

**1903**
Visits the White House to meet with President Teddy Roosevelt

Keller reads a book in braille to a group of blind children.

In 1924, Keller began working for the American Foundation for the Blind. She raised money that was used to help blind people get education and jobs.

**1904**

Graduates from Radcliffe College in Massachusetts, a state in the USA

**1920**

American women get the right to vote

**1924**

Begins work with the American Foundation for the Blind

In the early 1930s, US lawmakers were writing a new law to help disabled people. Keller pushed for the law to include the blind. She also worked to make braille the standard system of reading and writing for blind people.

When Keller met President Dwight Eisenhower in 1953, she touched his face to "see" his smile.

**1955**
Travels more than 40,000 miles across Asia to speak about fair treatment of disabled people

**1968**
Dies on June 1, aged 87

**1988**
Keller's family founds the Helen Keller Foundation for Research and Education

# Remembering Helen Keller

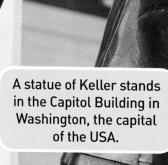

A statue of Keller stands in the Capitol Building in Washington, the capital of the USA.

Keller spent her life helping others. She helped to show the world how much disabled people could learn and do. Her work changed many lives for the better.

Keller died at her home on June 1, 1968. She was almost 88 years old. She is remembered for her hard work trying to make the world a better place for everyone.

## In Her Own Words

"The best and most beautiful things in the world cannot be seen or even touched – they must be felt with the heart."

# QUIZ WHIZ

**See how many questions you can get right!**
Answers are at the bottom of page 31.

**1**

**Where was Keller born?**

A. Alabama
B. New York
C. Washington, D.C.
D. Massachusetts

NEW YORK

MASSACHUSETTS

United States ★Washington, D.C.

ALABAMA

**2**

**How old was Keller when Annie Sullivan became her teacher?**

A. six years old
B. ten years old
C. one and a half years old
D. twenty years old

**What important event happened at the water pump?**

A. Keller had a drink of water.
B. Keller showed her teacher how to pump water.
C. Keller filled a bucket with water.
D. Keller learned the meaning of the word "water".

**3**

**4**

Keller learned braille so she could _____.

A. help her mother with chores around the house
B. read
C. play outside
D. tie her shoes

In 1902, Keller wrote _____.

A. her first book, *The Story of My Life*
B. the story of Annie Sullivan's childhood
C. a famous letter to her parents
D. her first comic book

**5**

**6**

As a suffragette, Keller believed women should have the right to _____.

A. get an education
B. get married
C. vote
D. drive a car

How did Keller help disabled people?

A. She wrote about the lives of disabled people.
B. She gave speeches about equal treatment.
C. She raised money to help the blind.
D. She did all of the above.

**7**

# Glossary

ALPHABET:

| | | | | | | | | |
|---|---|---|---|---|---|---|---|---|
| A | B | C | D | E | F | G | H | I |
| J | K | L | M | N | O | P | Q | R |
| S | T | U | V | W | X | Y | Z | |

**BRAILLE:** A reading system with raised dots that stand for letters and numbers

**DISABLED:** Having a condition that limits a person's ability to do something as others do

**FINGER-SPELL:** To communicate letters by making signs with the fingers

**SUFFRAGETTE:** A woman who works for the right of women to vote